and for too long after

Ellie White

and for too long after

Ellie White

AND FOR TOO LONG AFTER
Copyright©2019 Ellie White
All Rights Reserved
Published by Unsolicited Press
Printed in the United States of America.
First Edition.

All rights reserved. Printed in the United States of America. No part of this book may be used or reproduced in any manner whatsoever without written permission except in the case of brief quotations embodied in critical articles or reviews.

Attention schools and businesses: for discounted copies on large orders, please contact the publisher directly.

For information contact:
Unsolicited Press
Portland, Oregon
www.unsolicitedpress.com
orders@unsolicitedpress.com
619-354-8005

Cover Designer: Peter F. Lorën
Editor: Analieze Cervantes
Author Photo: Caroline Brae

ISBN: 978-1-950730-09-4

4am Aubade

I open my eyes to a wake
of shadows. In the street light's
distilled glow, dresses and shirts
hung to dry loom over the bed.

The still blades of the fan snatch
across the ceiling: a hand frozen
over something it had hoped to steal.
From the hallway, the red bird calls:

a shrill chirp, a warning
that something's about to break.
I feel last night's wine balloon
behind my forehead as I stand up.

I step across the threshold;
another sharp note ruptures. The pain
reverberates through my limbs, a legion
of hammers. The bird perches

talisman-like above the kitchen doorway.
I grope my way to the ladder leaning
beside the fridge. It opens with a grating
pop as I straddle its legs across the chasm

between kitchen and hallway. I climb up
to retrieve the bird, which comes quietly.
He lets me cup my hands around
his bloody feathers and carry him down.

Lacking a cage, I choose an empty cabinet.
I place the bird gently on one
of the lined shelves and close the door,
wait a few minutes to see if darkness

has tricked him into sleep. The silence
convinces me it has, and I slump
gratefully back to bed. In the street-
lit room, I stare at the ceiling.

The red bird perched on my chest
                              trills another warning.

I.

Indiana #1

It's just after one o'clock in the afternoon on the day after Christmas. We're somewhere west of Indianapolis, and my sister, Erin, is having a mini-crisis. I'm hesitantly reaching towards her, and seriously regretting my big mouth, as she screams "Get it out! Get it out!" Hindsight being a bitch, it only now occurs to me that I should have just waited until we were in the car to tell her. It's not like the situation is life-threatening. As it is, we're sitting in a booth at Steak 'n Shake, and I've just told my thirty-one-year-old sister that she has a gray hair. It's her first one and she is, understandably, flipping the hell out. The demon strand is about one inch from her hairline, just to the left of her off-center part.

Even with my detailed instructions, Erin couldn't find the hair to pull it out herself, which is how I ended up in my current predicament. She leans forward across the beige tabletop. I carefully separate the offending hair from its light brown companions and give it a sharp tug. It's a resistant little sucker and slips through my fingers the first time. But on the second try, I get it. This hair is strangely coarse, very shiny, and very, very gray. The fluorescent light lends it an attractive shimmer, and I can't resist rolling it between my fingers a few times.

Erin stares at me anxiously. It's starting to gross me out to have another person's hair in my hand, so I carefully pass the little monstrosity over to her.

"It's so weird looking! Plus, it's way thicker than my other hairs. Do you think it's a side effect of my new medication?"

"I don't know. Maybe."

The medication she's referring to is an antidepressant, so it's an unlikely culprit. But I'm trying to be supportive.

Erin despairingly holds the hair up to the light. I start glancing around. It doesn't seem like anyone's noticed the dramatic scene that just took place at our table. But considering I had to wait ten minutes in line for the bathroom, and no less than two toddlers stuck their heads under the door while I was going, I'm not surprised. It's a busy day at a cheap family restaurant, so everyone has their own shit to pay attention to (no pun intended).

Aside from the scrawny teenager sitting at the end of a table of ten who's sticking a red straw through one of his gauged-out ears, there isn't anything interesting for me to look at. Just people in generic clothing talking and chasing kids around. Steak 'n Shakes are all the same: black and white tiled floors, red pleather seat cushions, and cheesy neon signs with things like "Takhomasak" on them.

For people who didn't grow up with them, the uniformity of chain restaurants like Steak 'n Shake tends to be horrifying. But for people like Erin and me, who spent a decent chunk of our childhood in the Midwest, some of these restaurants have sentimental value. Until they passed away in 2007, we spent every Christmas with our maternal grandparents at their house in Indianapolis. At some point during each visit, the whole family (aunts, uncles, cousins, and occasionally, guests) would pile into two or three cars and go to Steak 'n Shake for lunch. Even after eight years, it doesn't feel right for Erin and me to pass through Indy and not eat here.

Tracing a Scar

From the big window, I can only see the ground. Frozen raindrops litter the grass like spilled rice. My sister and I are playing hide and go seek. Dad sits upstairs watching basketball on the good TV. I crawl across the dark red carpet and slip behind the couch, the red and white striped fabric itching against the side of my face. My sister, who was watching the hail outside, now shrieks *I didn't say go yet! You have to come back out!* She's older than me, so I have to listen. I crawl back around the couch, forgetting about the coffee table on the other side. A sharp corner scrapes across my left eyebrow and it feels like getting a shot, a sting deep under my skin. I roll on the floor, pressing my hand over my eye. Now, my sister really screams, and I hear Dad's gigantic feet on the stairs.

He shouts, too. I cry because I know I'm in trouble, but I don't know why he's handing me a washcloth full of ice when it's winter outside, or why we all have to get in the car. Everything goes so fast. Dad is still yelling at me as he's driving. He reaches back with his long arm and grabs my hand that's holding the washcloth. He presses it on my eyebrow hard saying *Hold it there!* As soon as he turns around, I drop it on the floor. The ice is too cold; the cloth drips with someone's blood.

Indiana #2

After thoroughly examining the silver-gray hair, Erin sets it down on the black part of her paper placemat and takes out her iPhone to snap a picture. Then, she starts looking for something in her dark blue purse to wrap the hair in so she can save it. I have no fucking clue why she wants to save it. It seems pretty disgusting, and besides, she has the picture. I almost want to ask her what she's planning to do with the hair when she gets back home, but decide against it. She's still obviously distressed and I don't want to piss her off. Eventually, she finds an unused front pocket to stash it in, and a few minutes later, our food arrives.

I have my usual grilled cheese and cheese fries, and Erin has some new spicy steak-burger. We both take comfort food seriously, so we spend most of the meal in silence. In the absence of good people-watching or conversation, my thoughts keep drifting back to the hair. Most people hate everything to do with getting old: crow's feet, sagging skin, creaking joints, teeth you have to take out at night. After all, getting old means eventually dying. Who wants to think about that shit? Much better to start planning your first skydive (which you'll never go through with) or designing a new exercise plan (which you'll never follow), than to sit around facing the reality that your body isn't going to last forever.

This is probably what motivated Erin to scream at me to rip out the hair, despite the old adage that four or ten or however many more would grow in its place. What separates Erin in this situation from the average person who doesn't want to die is that she chose to save the hair. She couldn't handle it being on her head, but she also wasn't willing to condemn it to total annihilation. It was something she wanted to hide from other people, but perhaps not something she needed to hide from herself.

If this is true, then Erin's gray hair is like the tiny permanent creases I've noticed forming between my eyebrows, the ones I can't quite bring myself to hate, though I know it's the socially encouraged thing to do. I think I feel a certain affection for my future frown lines because, in my mind, death is part of the past, not part of the future. I actually find the idea of getting older comforting. Though I rarely think of myself as being grown up (there are always at least three kinds of candy on my nightstand), I honestly never planned to be around this long. I never planned to see my older sister get her first gray hair. I never even planned on turning eighteen. At fourteen years old, I sat in a Steak 'n Shake dipping shoestring fries in cheddar cheese sauce the exact same way I am right now, except I was surrounded by most of my extended family. It was the day after Christmas, and I was thinking about how I'd do it.

I'd tried slitting my wrists before, but I could never find anything sharp enough. Or maybe, I was just too much of a pain wimp to press that hard. Either way, opening a vein was out. Shooting myself would be simple, except I didn't know a single person who owned a gun, and even if I did, I didn't know how to use one. Asphyxiation just seemed like way too much fucking work. I would have to get into the attic of our house to find a strong enough beam to hang from, and then there was the whole matter of finding a rope or something that wouldn't snap. Driving off a cliff was out, too. I lived in one of the flattest places on Earth. Plus, I was too young to drive. Pills seemed like the way to go. I'd read online that you could use any of the over-the-counter pain medicines, as long you made sure to take enough. Three years later, when I was seventeen, I finally took enough.

Wishes

August, 2003

The medicine cabinet was filled with my grandmother's linen tablecloths and crocheted doilies. The light blue pills were cocooned moths. When I swallowed them, they emerged from their chrysalises and flew away into the warm cave of my chest. Dim-sighted, they couldn't tell my bones and organs from the shadows. My mother did not scream as she grabbed the phone from my hand, and so the ambulance never arrived. The paramedics were not worried when I refused the ride. The economy had recently collapsed and our currency was worthless, so my mother never asked me where we were going to get six thousand dollars. Our dog didn't exist, and wasn't let out. Also, the refrigerator was broken, so there were no groceries to put away. We left for the hospital, which turned out to be a large canvas tent in the Brazilian rainforest immediately. It was 95 degrees in there. When the saline hit my stomach, it wasn't cold. The doctor's brother hadn't coaxed his Corvette off a cliff six months ago, so I didn't have to listen to the story as he rinsed my insides out.

All this time, the moths were sound asleep. I couldn't bear to wake them, so I never threw up the empty cocoons. There was no activated charcoal. My stomach didn't balloon like an angry blister. My skin didn't ache from stretching, and I never spent two days vomiting chalky tar. In 1998, talk therapy was formally abandoned as an acceptable practice. I didn't have to make a counseling appointment before I left the tent. Also, my mother didn't let me skip it two weeks later. Eventually, the moths grew so large I had to unzip my side and let them go.

Upside-down Girl

In the foyer, she greets you with a smile,
blue eyes bright, nose slightly crinkled,
as if she were about to giggle.
Her mouth is small, the lips tiny
petals curved gently around
a stigma of broken teeth.

Absently, she picks at a stitch
in her forehead, her fingers
mangled stems growing
from an impossibly childish palm.
She doesn't speak, but extends
her free hand. She wants

your candle. When you don't
hand it over, she rips the stitch,
deftly pulling thread out
of the seam along her hairline.
You hold the candle tighter, step
backward. She peels away
her grin. Faceless,

she lunges forward and grabs
the candle, uses it to set fire
to her wheat-brown hair,
her shattered teeth now the eye
of a blazing dahlia.

When her dress ignites,
she convulses with laughter.

Above, the chandelier swings
with the rhythm of her writhing body,
her delicate feet tangled in brassy tentacles.

Indiana #3

I watch my sister eat a stray slice of jalapeño from her plate, trying to convince myself that after eleven years, she's surely forgiven me. I'm pretty sure I've forgiven myself. In any case, I'm here now. A server in black pants and a white button-up shirt—standard Steak 'n Shake garb— comes over with the two milkshakes we ordered forty-five minutes ago. She's middle-aged and looks about as miserable as most people who work in restaurants. She doesn't apologize for the shakes being late. She just strides away, her slightly over-processed blonde ponytail swinging. I poke a straw into my chocolate-covered strawberry malt while wondering if my existence here at this moment is a way of making amends. After all, I sincerely do consider death to be a thing of the past, even if that past is not always so distant.

Dear River,

I have always been good
at holding my breath, cycling the same
gasp of air from lungs, to mouth, to lungs...

Dear Wall, your safety seems dubious at best.
I don't doubt the quality of your concrete,
the soundness of your structure, or the hands
of those who wrestled you into being.
I suspect the hearts involved were ordinary, at worst.
I confess, I don't usually think in three dimensions
or recognize the sad lack of symmetry in sidewalk slabs.
My mistrust rests on a far less solid foundation
than your bricks. It is a voice, gentle as the waves lapping
at your side. It bids me to come closer,
to lean my back against your cool strength.

Dear River, I'm not sure if this salt on my skin
is yours or if it's just sweat. I'm not sure
if the salt of my body is the same as the salt
in the sea. I don't know where salt
comes from. I only know it lives
in my blood, which I sometimes crave
to feel on my skin like sweat.

Dear Wall, despite your continued willingness
to support my spine, I feel
that obnoxious sleeping-on-an-airplane wobble

starting to warp my neck into a swinging
handle. My head, as it snaps back, feels
more mallet than flesh and bone. When
you and I meet with an exquisite thud, my brain
suddenly feels more rubber than steel. This betrayal,
and the blood that never comes of it, make me
think Dear Hope is a transient bricklayer,
a builder of walls that must be maintained by those
who need them. And so I hold this salty blood in my body:
a deserted wall restraining a swollen river: a set of lungs
      recycling air.

How to Lie to Your Mother

Talk about your cats. You're worried
the calico is getting too thin, but she
won't eat any of the food you bought,
not even the organic one. Mention
you're redecorating your bedroom.
You don't have a favorite color
at the moment, so you picked blue.
You've spray-painted some wall hangings
and you found this paisley print sheet
at Thrift Store USA. You're going to make
curtains. Everything is blue.
Say you can't wait to visit her.

Insist on a trip to IKEA. It's so close
and you need shelves. You don't want
your new roommate to think
you're a slob. Dodge the question
about group therapy. Ask her
about her health. She always
has a lot to say about it.
Try to remember which medications
have changed. There's a list
in her purse, but still, someone should
know what she's taking. Dad doesn't.
Has it been thirty minutes yet?

You can't talk for less or she'll feel
shut out. Ask about the animals
at the shelter. Are there any new kittens?
Try to stay focused on the details
when she describes them. Make it
into a game. See how much
you remember later. Check the clock
again. Wait for her to lose
her train of thought. Pretend
you've just realized what time it is.
Tell her you need to get ready for work.
Say I love you. Say goodbye.

How to Hide
for J.P.

Get out of bed and find the good
scissors. The red ones.
Go out to the porch.
Take down all of the wind-
chimes. Dismember them.
Go back inside. Open
the closets. Bring out
all the jackets and shoes.
Tie up every lace and string
until there are only perfect
bows. Put it all away
and pry open the pendulum
clock. Remove the weights.
They'll make good bookends.
Go to the window. Let down
the blinds and then snip off
the extra cord. Do this in every room.
Consider buying darker curtains,
not because you no longer love
light, but because you never know
what will cast a swinging shadow.

You Were an Interesting Case

i. Going In

The day you looked Death in the face and told it
to fuck all the way off,
a pretty counselor walked beside you through the student
    center.
The police kindly kept their distance until you arrived
at the car, where the older one helped you fasten your
    seatbelt
across the gray plastic seat. It was so low,
you barely had to scrunch down.
At the hospital, a nurse took your vitals, and then led you
through a series of push-button doors.
On opening, each one leaned awkwardly away from its
    partner.
The nurse left you in the observation area and after a while,
the counselor left, too.
A new nurse came and drew your blood. Then, a different
    one came
with pizza and French fries. The dessert, of course,
was unidentifiable and your roommate laughed at it when
    he popped by
to say hello. The food nurse wanted a urine sample.
Though you'd never been arrested,
the bathroom reminded you of jail. The steel toilet was
    smeared
with shit. The handicap rails sported brown handprints.

You thought it best not to complain.
Like a good student, you answered every question, called
    your family, even emailed
your study partner. Angry and rejected, Death looked on.
You both cried a little bit.
Eventually, you were taken upstairs.

ii. The Red Woman

Long before Death came into the picture, she was there. The Red Woman: a pure and vivacious rage. On a long and drunken walk home last April, she slipped into your shoe like a pebble from the riverbank. Your mind slid into her like a warm bath. She said *Break the mirror. Punch the wall.* and your body obeyed. The next morning, you could only finger the bruises as you watched the coffee brew. Summer was a blur. She'd show up, sometimes empty-handed, sometimes with a bottle of cheap Pinot, and the world was only corners. Only knives, and walls, and mirrors, and morning after morning with dried blood and Mr. Coffee. You didn't bother with band aids or explanations. In late July, you finally let her move in, even got a new tattoo to mark the occasion: a keyhole on your ribs, so she could see out. But when she invited Death into your bed last night, you knew they both had to go. You didn't know she was here at the hospital until a disheveled woman in a blue nightgown wandered into your supposedly safe room at 5 a.m. Under a blanket that reeked of sour spit, greasy scalps, and piss, you pretended to be asleep. She muttered *White bitches. Why are all these white bitches lying in these beds? Just lying. I will set this whole place on fire. I'll burn every last one of these white bitches up.*

iii. Humor

In the event you should like to make a joke,
ask to borrow the red marker. Use it to carefully color in
the letters on your milk carton. Try to imagine you are
    climbing
the hills of the M, or perhaps they are sand dunes,
or snow drifts. You haven't been outside
in four days. It's meditation hour,
so the television screen in the activity room is taunting you
with piney forests, austere mountain lakes, fields of
    wildflowers, and random deer.
The accompanying music is of the "serene" variety
usually reserved for acupuncturist's offices.
Speaking of needles, you got this milk carton from an
    addict.
He drinks at least three milks with every meal,
but has no teeth so it's hard to tell if he's absorbing the
    calcium.
In his honor, and the Red Woman's too, if you're being
    honest, you add
a festive drop of blood just beneath
the straddled legs of the K. You show it first
to the friendly old man who almost killed his brother-in-
    law last week.
You tell him *Hey look, it's milk for vampires.*
Then, you turn to the bearded woman coloring a butterfly
    who recently mistook her chest
for a knife block and say *Got any Kotex?*
I think the K sprung a leak.

On the screen, an unidentifiable farm animal (goat? sheep?)
        grazes
near the base of an oak tree. Behind it, gray mountains rise
like the constant prayers of the pregnant sex worker sitting
        one table over.
Nobody laughs. It's not that kind of joke.

iv. Valium/Atarax

The Lord doesn't speak to you like he did to your cousin. Instead, you watch from the flooded floor of the shower room as the Red Woman slithers aboard the dark ship, the one that carried Tennyson's good King Arthur away. She is a serpent with an apple in her belly. Or maybe she is a ghost like the king. The king is still here somewhere, though poor Sir Bedivere has long since gone home to his grief. The Red Woman rocks with the ship; the night and the water indistinguishable from sleep. She once said she was heartless, so you lent her yours. She returned it seemingly intact save for a single splinter, bright and growing like a winter's dawn. In the galley, the Red Woman taps her foot on a rotting floor, and somehow, this translates as a pulse. She begins to dance a waltz, her bare blue feet finding every corner, brown toenails snapping off one by one, and your mind becomes the air in a car speeding past a country graveyard, prickly and full of gasps.

v. Diagnosis and Discharge

Praise the three wise doctors,
for they have given it a name,
and that name has been fruitful
and multiplied. Now, there's a word
for the days you spent drifting in and out
on the couch, binge-watching BBC period dramas
and forgetting to eat. A word
for the first two weeks of every quarter
in junior year when you never stopped.
Best of all, a pair of words for the intolerable sharpness,
the screaming thoughts and tapping fingers,
the toe-stubbing agony of sitting through lecture classes.
With this new vocabulary came little white pills,
each one a pure and perfect prayer to stop
the swinging. This is what they sent you home with.
Your mother met you on the other side of the doors,
and you let her hug you, let her see
her youngest and most difficult child
still intact. Your apartment looked like it did
five days ago. True to their nature, the cats purred
as they wound their steadfast and thready love around your
    feet.
The nose ring they made you take out
slid back in with minimal fuss.
You took a long shower,
conditioned your hair, put on nice deodorant.
You'd missed yourself too much to put on clothes,
so you crawled into bed naked. While you lay there

watching *Girl, Interrupted* and realizing no one
would believe any of this happened,
Death and the Red Woman sat in your kitchen.

II.

Croagh Patrick #1

About halfway up the mountain, the air feels thinner. If this were another day, another trip, it might be okay to turn around, to accept that Croagh Patrick was the wrong choice for a first mountain. But not on my 29th birthday, not with 30 looming just around the corner, and definitely not in the midst of a study abroad course I'll be paying for till I'm 45. That kind of a copout would never sit well with the stubborn, Scottish blood pounding against my temples. I stare up the trail, squinting to see through the thick mist. The rocky slope I'm trudging up seems to shift. I lose my balance and begin looking for a good spot to stop for a breather. I stumble up a few more feet, the toes of my boots catching on protruding stones, before deciding to just brace my feet in the mud and wait for the scenery to stop spinning. There's a steep drop on my right side. At the bottom, white-tipped waves roll across a teal blue sea.

Fortune: chance, hap, or luck, an adventure, a mishap, a disaster, to run a risk.

Atop a rope, my seven-year-old body spins. I'm high above the gymnasium, pretending the blue mats below are a rectangular sea. I grip the well-used but still rough rope just above the red electrical tape that serves as a finish line. I'm only using my hands. I keep my legs stretched out, cartwheel- straight, below me. My pointed toes draw circles like an aerial Spirograph. My body orbits the rope. Every movement, every breath, an act of trust.

Croagh Patrick #2

I've asked a few hikers on their way down how far the top is, and the consensus is forty-five minutes. It's taking nearly all my concentration to keep from falling. The incline increases by the minute, and my quadriceps have been burning for so long the pain doesn't register any more. My legs just feel stiff and uncooperative. I look around at some of the fitter hikers who are still obviously struggling and realize once again the magnitude of what I've taken on. I haven't set foot inside a gym for years. I consider walking to class to be aerobic. The idea that I will have to use stairs at some point tomorrow is extremely distressing. But this is no time to get caught up in worries. The rocks are slimy, the damp gravelly dirt offers zero traction, and though the landscape has finally stopped spinning, it's starting to feel like I am.

Staying ██ After Discharge

1. Work with your ████████████████████████ illness ████ Learn ████████ self-management. Read books and ████ people ████ use every imaginable source ████████████

2. Accept ████████████████████ a long, painful and difficult ████████████ recovery. Accept that it's ██ your fault

3. Take ██ responsibility ████████████████

4. Guard your ████████████████ sleep

5. Learn ████████████████ which stresses are the most difficult ████████████ to manage

6. ████████ Make ████████████ life ██ predictable

7. Evaluate your ████████ limitations ████████████████ (for this week, for this month) ████ (for this year, for your lifetime). Enlist ████████ your

███████████████████████ friends and family in this process.

8. Join a self-help group. ███████████████
   █████████

9. Take your medications █████ If you're unhappy
   ████████████████ but by all means don't make changes ██████████ by yourself.

10. Ask for help ████████████

11. Be honest ████████ withhold anything █████
    ████████ you know is important.

12. ████████████ Discuss ██████ alcohol with your therapist.█

13. Recovery ████████████████ often isn't ██████ patient ████████████████ there will be ups and downs.

14. Make a plan with your █████ friends and family █████
    ████████████████ (this is called relapse).
    If a relapse can be █████████ dealt with █████
    aggressively, it can usually be ████████ prevented
    altogether. Make a █████████ list of
    signs, █████████ plan █████ to reduce
    █████ structure and support when █████████ signs occur.

The Aran Islands

I'm lost on Inishmaan—separated from my group—for nearly thirty minutes. I catch up with them at the ruins of a house. Seeing the outlines of my classmates against the hazy blue sky as I perch atop the rock wall of a pasture produces a relief so strong it tingles through all my limbs. Yet, it doesn't seem anyone noticed my absence. Most of the group is standing about ten feet above me on the walls of the house. Three of the walls have flat tops, but one comes to a sharp peak. It looks like a chimney may have been there once. I scale one of the walls to join my classmates. The surface on top is about two feet wide, but it's necessary to walk carefully because a lot of the rocks are loose. Even though I've seen hundreds of these walls in the last day or so that we've been on the island, their construction still amazes me.

One of the guys has climbed up the chimney wall. He sits on the flat stone on top posing like a king. Immediately, I know I want to go up there. I ask who else has gone up, and it seems four or five people have done it successfully. It looks dangerous, but that only increases my resolve. I've been taking chances like crazy on this trip, trying to scare myself into a good thrill buzz. But even when I snuck away at the Cliffs of Moher to climb onto a narrow, windy ledge and swing my feet over the sea two hundred meters below, I barely felt anything.

A Show-Off's Lament
The National Gallery, Dublin, 2015

Twenty-four photos of the Aran Islands
surround me. On my knees,
the bruises from Inishmaan
not yet faded. In my backpack,
a shredded pair of denim leggings:
I remember them catching on the edge
of a flat stone atop a ruined chimney.
The stone tipped with half of me
still on it; the rocks under my feet shifted.
Fifteen feet below, the ground gaped
with hungry stones. I made
a strange sound, almost primitive,
like a whimper. The rocks stared
up at me. All of them waiting.

Croagh Patrick #3

    The hikers passing on their way down now say it's only twenty minutes. It's slow going since my legs often aren't long enough to use the footholds I see other people using. Though there are tall people in my family, we aren't really a long-legged bunch. At 5'2," short legs can be a considerable inconvenience. It's unfathomable to me how anyone could carry something heavier than my small backpack full of snacks and water, yet several of the people who've overtaken me on this climb have been carrying large packs. They're the kind you would use if you were on a backpacking trip, with those padded straps that go around the front of your hips. A siren red one on the back of a young blonde man passes me. It even has straps to attach a tent on top, though he isn't carrying one. I stare at the backpack's shape disappearing ahead of me, a cardinal flying away, and recall I haven't set foot in a tent in almost six years.

Dyspareunia: Ode to the Pudendal Nerve

I crawled into bed with the smell of the river still in my hair, silt pressed into the soles of my feet, ash smeared across my skin. I was too tired to shower. Still drunk, but aware of a dull ache in my hands. I'd clung to the steering wheel the whole way home, scanning the pre-dawn darkness for cops. There had been no other choice. I didn't want to leave the tent, the campsite, my brand-new bottle of sunscreen. When I spoke, I don't know what I said, only that he wouldn't stop shouting. At some point, he climbed over me and sat on the damp ground to smoke.

I lay there like a fist. My body clenched around the sharp shadow of a knife. He'd seemed shocked when he rolled away from me. His chest hair scraped over my right breast, and I realized I'd said *stop*. The blade was now slick and dripping like a sun-rotted fish. When it was inside me, it had been so small: a blood spile: the sting of a paper wasp. How did this begin?

Separated from myself, I watched us duck into the tent; watched as we crawled in circles, feeling for the air mattress; watched his body press flat against mine: a lily pad on water. I'd been planning it for weeks, hoping so badly that the doctors were wrong, that it wouldn't hurt, that I could still make this choice. We'd downed two six-packs on the river bank, watched the sky explode, the ash floating down all around us. I barely knew him. It was the Fourth of July.

Croagh Patrick #4

The last time I went into a tent, I thought I knew what was going to happen. I didn't love or want him; I wanted sex. Maybe that's why the moment he thrust his hips downward, I felt a searing pain. I was being sliced open, shredded, ripped apart. Something was eating me alive from the inside out. At twenty-three, I was far from being a virgin, but my body had never done this before. It had never rejected a man. I stared helplessly into his slate blue eyes, begging him to stop. Eventually, he did.

I think he expected me to call him the next day, but I didn't. The clinic said the wound inside me was the size of a quarter, a blood blister of sorts. I pictured it: a plum red balloon. A week later, I heard he'd been bragging to his friends about fucking me. Still, I didn't call. I knew he wanted retaliation, needed to know he had some kind of power over me. To prove him wrong, I threw myself into school. I don't remember much from Philosophy or Geology, but I remember learning to convert pain into energy. I learned how to not feel the parts of me that hurt, how to fill those gaps with knowledge. Though I no longer think I see his old blue truck in traffic or catch his scent in grocery store aisles, a part of me still thinks if I go into a tent, he'll be waiting.

Vanishing Below the Waist
Union Station, Washington D.C., 2013

Standing in line
to get off the train,
the door separating
this car from its siblings
closes against my hip.
Smoking behind a pillar
by the tour buses,
a bold brindled bird
pecks my boot. As I perch
in a metal cubicle,
the automatic toilet flushes
beneath me. I glance
down at the pale blue panties
stretched ungracefully
across my thighs,
and see five dark hairs
have been ripped out,
the bulb-like follicles
still attached. I wonder
how I did not feel this.

St. Agatha Waits for Peter
The National Gallery, Edinburgh, 2015

It's true. I did not need
them, the mounds of flesh
where my children should have
fed, their milk teeth nibbling
cracked skin, suckling little drops of
blood with every gulp of milk.
Still, as I lie bleeding,
my breasts carried away in a bowl
(perhaps given to a hungry dog)
I want them back. I send a prayer
like a stumbling child to heaven.
I wait in the blooming red.

Croagh Patrick #5

Ten minutes from the top, the mist is so thick it feels like being inside a cloud. I can see the path, but not much else. I'm not sure if the incline is steeper here or if it's just that I'm exhausted, but I'm seriously struggling. I lose my balance for what feels like the millionth time and catch myself making that involuntary whimpering sound I made two days ago on Inishmaan. A few of the hikers around me hear it. A middle-aged man with graying hair climbs sideways across the path to get next to me. He offers me a helping hand, but I assure him I'm all right. I've yet to actually fall down on this hike, though I keep coming close. I've become an expert at swaying back and forth with my arms out.

"Are you sure?" the man asks. His blue-gray eyes try to home in on any uncertainty in my green ones. I say "Yeah. I'm fine. I'm just a clumsy hiker." He and his companions overtake me as I continue to make my way slowly up the slippery path. It's hard for me to accept help, even when I could clearly use it. If there's even the slightest chance that I can do something myself, I'll always try that first.

Assist: to stand to or by; to be present.

I'm frozen on the uneven bars. Both my hands and one foot rest on top of the lower bar, but the second foot points at the blue mat. I'm eleven and painfully aware of how awkward I look in this position. My spotter, a muscular young man with brown hair and hazel eyes, places his hand on my back. *It's okay. You can do it. I'm not going to let you fall.* But I don't believe him. Can't believe him. I am faithless. This has never happened before, but it will happen every time from now on. In this moment, it seems all the broken promises from my short life have suddenly caught up with me.

Paper Dolls

The dining room table looks like wood,
but isn't. My sister and I sit folding
paper tabs around paper bodies.

The dresses are strange puffy-sleeved affairs,
their full skirts unlike anything
we've ever worn. We fold in silence,

my five-year-old fingers struggling
with the tiny creases. My sister is older,
faster. But her shoulders are tensed.

In the back bedroom,
mom shouts into the phone, calls Dad
a sonofabitch. The phone slams

into the receiver. We hear
furious steps heading our way.
As mom appears in the doorway,

my sister slips under her seat cushion.
I catch in the ceiling
fan's breeze and flutter away.

Visiting
for Lulu

It's the middle of the night. I lie awake
and restless, struggling to sleep in a strange house,
in a child's room. The wall beside me
is plastered with coloring book pages. My feet:

catacombed by dolls. The room's residents, two
little girls, sleep beneath me. I hear
a muffled whimper. A tiny sob. So weak,
and yet, the sound feels like it's been pulled

straight through my body: like smoke,
or a thunderclap; then, stillness.
The room's atmosphere is suddenly clay.
My sprawled body presses into it

like a mold. The sound comes again.
This time, a cluster of smothered yelps.
Still pinned to my mattress, the ceiling
less than two feet from my face, I wonder

what the dream is about. Once, I dreamed
of my mother nine feet tall and skinless,
a walking length of muscle chasing me
through our house; her head: a red balloon.

She Was a Wild Mother(fucker)
The National Gallery, Dublin, 2015

The dark-haired little girl has brought flowers. Playfully, she runs her fingertips across the soles of her sleeping mother's feet. The mother sits up in surprise. Just before she sees her sweet child, the flowers, just before the mother smiles, her eyes flash: a feral cat's.

Losing Respect
Hot Springs, Arkansas, 2002

Sometimes, disbelief is a hydra:
new explanations sprouting to replace
the disproven. It can take years
for the evidence to sink in, a cacophony
of whispers, endless rows of averted eyes
like the teeth of some great shark,
the newly familiar clink of glass
bottles as you tip the trash can back
before rolling it down to the curb.

Or it can happen with one flick
of a lighter. I took my first drag
in front of my father outside the NA
meeting where he got his fourth
thirty-day chip. Dad didn't get angry,
didn't snatch the Turkish Jade
from my fingers, didn't stamp
it out on the pavement. I was fifteen.

He looked down at his size twelves,
this photograph of a tall man who used
to live in my house, who always forgot
and tripped over the dog bowls,
and in the slightest rendition
of his booming voice, said
You don't have to do that.

But it was too late: both of us
undone, in that moment,
and for too long after.

Crying at the Victoria and Albert Museum of Childhood
London, 2015

A broken dollhouse sits on a shelf
in my parents' basement, cobalt blue
with white trim. It's been torn
off its base, the carved porch posts
split, splintered. I can't let it go.
I used to make plans to fix it,
add carpet and wallpaper, find some
corner of the living room to display it.

I remember watching Dad build it,
cussing sometimes at the tiny nails.
The paint and wood glue stank up
the basement and gave Mom a headache.
Dad made me make choices; stairs
or window frames, plain porch posts
or carved ones, one or the other,
not both. Sweat dripped
from his forehead while he worked
to build me this thing. I can't let go.

It's the only project we ever worked on
together, the only evidence that he
might've liked me as a kid; sometimes,
at least. I sit in front of a museum case
where a blue dollhouse is on display,

catch my own reflection in the glass.
It looks away as the image blurs.

Idiom

I feel the familiar chill of limestone
on my skin when he says
I'm an easy dog to hunt with.
I know he isn't from Arkansas,
doesn't drive a '91 Bronco with broken
turn signals, has never been swimming
in West Fork creek. He does carry a gun,
but it's not the twelve-gauge that rusted
in my living room closet
during the winter of '04.

All I can say is, *I lived in the Ozarks*,
but he doesn't understand.
He only sees mountains and trees,
not the November day when that truck,
the gun, an Arkansan boy, and me
went up on Sugar Mountain to look
for turkey. It was a minor accident,
a mishandled turn that launched us

into an oak. I was wearing my seatbelt,
but the boy wasn't and his head made
a thumping sound when it struck the wheel.
The loaded gun fell out of his lap,
but didn't fire. It wasn't until
I picked it up later that I saw
he'd already turned off the safety.

Croagh Patrick #6

I'm beginning to wish I'd accepted that stranger's help. The top is so close, probably less than five minutes, but there aren't any other hikers near me, and the possibility of falling is especially worrisome. It would suck to be injured and have to wait for someone to pass by. So far in my life, I've been lucky in that regard. Despite my inability to trust other people, and my general hard-headedness, I've yet to find myself seriously hurt and alone.

There's something thrilling about climbing a steep, slippery slope by yourself, knowing that the stakes are high, but there's a funny sort of sadness about it, too. When you refuse other people's help long enough, it stops feeling like a choice. It starts to feel like you've always been this way, like you were born a fortress, like there's never been another way to exist except cut off from everyone else. I'm not sure if it's the thin air or my emotions, but the lump forming in my throat feels about the size of the small boulder I just crawled over.

The Doorway

Brace your feet against the baseboards.
Feel your palms slip across
the paint's pink satin finish.

Use every muscle in your ten-
year-old body to keep the door
closed. Know you are strong.

On the other side, she snaps
her jaw, charges the door
again and again.

Her nails scrape merely an inch
from your spine. You hear wood
splintering, smell her matted fur.

A grating snarl escapes your throat,
filling your mouth with salt.
Of course, you are hers.

I Have Scaled These City Walls

On a picnic bench in the Pieman Café, I sit confused, my loneliness disproportionate to the situation. It's just one night in the Times Hostel in Dublin, one night in a room of strange girls who haven't said a word to me or each other all afternoon. I've finished my pie and mash, and know I should leave, but U2's "Still Haven't Found What I'm Looking For" comes on the radio and I stay to listen to it. It reminds me of my mom's car. Mom went on a U2 kick the year I turned fifteen. We must've listened to *The Joshua Tree* a hundred times.

Staring out the window at the narrow street which leads into Temple Bar, I feel the song's connection to my current predicament. On this month-long trip through Scotland, Ireland, and England, it feels like I'm searching for something. I keep looking for rules to break, acting half my age, trying to terrify myself into some kind of catharsis.

Groups of young people in every imaginable type of clothing pass by. I think about my sister, my traveling companion through Scotland, whom I said goodbye to in Edinburgh two days ago. It's not so much her as a person that I miss; I just miss not feeling alone. It's damp and chilly outside, just like it was in Edinburgh and Glasgow. Still, it feels different here. I know I need to go back to the hostel, so I get up and pay the friendly brunette behind the counter before heading out into the light rain.

Croagh Patrick #7

The view from the top was incredible. A small group of my classmates were waiting to sing "Happy Birthday" to me as I hiked the final few feet. It was unexpected and sort of silly, but exactly what I needed after my brief bout of the lonelies. There was a grave and an eerie old church up there, and hikers in red and yellow rain jackets sat eating lunch on its steps. Looking down through the mist, I saw a small island just off the coast. Gray clouds smudged across the tops of its small hills.

I'm glad the view was worth it, because getting down is proving to be even harder than climbing up. I saw a lot of hikers slipping and sliding when I was going up, and I suspected it wouldn't be easy. Still, it's amazing how few places there are to put my feet, and how quickly the gravel gives way. I literally can't stand still. My heart isn't racing and I've stopped sweating, but my leg muscles are cramping hard. I can feel my left knee starting to give out. I hurt it during my escapades at the Cliffs of Moher, and it hasn't forgiven me yet. I hesitate above a particularly steep section of the descent, and another man stops to try to help me. He's probably in his fifties or sixties, with grayish white hair and a beard. When he offers me his hand, I force myself to take it. I can do that now sometimes.

Brave: courageous, daring, intrepid, stout-hearted.

We sit in his car at the beginning of a footpath into the swamp. I say, for the first time, "I'm scared." He says quietly, "I only want to hurt you how you want to be hurt." It's the same thing he said two months ago when we first started chatting online. We get out of the car. I follow him down the path, focusing on the rhythm of my footsteps and the throbbing blood in my ears. I think of climbing the rope in gym class as a child, try to remember what it felt like to trust my hands, to trust the air, to trust fortune. I think of the spotter in gymnastics class, how suddenly and inexplicably my faith in him had vanished, how after a while, mistrust feels like a second skin.

When we stop in a clearing, I look around nervously. A squirrel rustles in the alder trees, and I shiver. I've never done this outside before, never even tried it with anyone but my first boyfriend. He asks, "Are you ready?" and I nod and walk slowly toward him, yellow leaves crunching under my feet. I don't remember if he said anything else, but I remember him putting his hand on my back, helping me to stay in position. The first strike lands so quickly I don't have time to brace myself. In retrospect, I'm grateful he didn't make me wait. I don't think I could've waited. I drive home slowly, spend the afternoon rotating ice packs, hoping to be healed. Not by the pain he's inflicted, but by the trust it took for me to let him do it, a trust he didn't break.

Ode to an Unhaunting

I learned kink // is another word for survival. learned to love / the body more for what it can do / than for what it is… to break / is to be sanctified.
                              –Marty McConnell

The path into the swamp is a maze of footbridges. His steps and yours fall into a syncopated but familiar rhythm. You pause to brush off a moth. Ahead, he hesitates at a fork, trying to remember the way to the outlook, someplace with a bench. Black marble deer eyes peer through the trees. Eventually, you find a good spot.

★

This house is a tree cemetery.
All I want is to take a shower,
but the pipes run sap. Once, I was
glued to the floor. I don't want it
to happen again. Everything outside
is so bloody. It stains my feet,
creeps up my dress, makes me
a blooming wound. The wind,
frigid witch, never stops moaning.

★

The struggle is brief, but necessary, like introducing oneself to an instrument. Though he knows your body, he must still seize control. He sits on the edge of the bench, his grip on your wrists tightening. He yanks you down hard. Your elbow knocking against a wooden edge interrupts the otherwise fluid motion. He asks if you're okay. Then, it begins.

The first slap catches you off guard. You suck the thick, muggy air through your teeth. But soon, your breath matches the staccato of skin on skin, two bodies making one sound.

*

The Red Woman is always
my enemy. The bedroom sloshes
like wine in my glass.
There is never enough
wine. The knock, knock, knock-
ing of my skull against the wall
is all that's real. Skin collects
under my nails. I wait
for the blood to surface,
wait to breathe. Tonight,
everything is a weapon.
Tonight, I don't stop.

*

You are standing, your livid knuckles gripping the wooden railing, toes curling into the grain of the planked floor. You fight to stay in your body, but the sound makes you forget.

Forget you are in a swamp. Forget the light rain, rustling trees, sharp smell of brackish water. Forget the bruises blooming beneath your skin. Forget how long it took you to trust him. Grip the railing. Hold still.

Each lick of leather on skin: two quarter notes. The air singing as it's sliced. Hiss. Snap. Whish. Pop. You begin to measure your gasps in 4/4 time.

*

I remember a deep blue walk,
a cocktail party of haints, then
a slipping under. Seconds numb
with grief, inches creaking by.
I kicked and kicked, stormed
every door I could find.
I was skull-weary, starving,
stashed away beneath the living
room floor. I breathed
only in screams. I breathed.

*

The second time he takes your wrists in his hand, and pulls you down, it is gentle. You are self- conscious, but not afraid. You stare at the evenly spaced lines of murky water between the slats of the walkway, liniment stinging your welted skin. Then, he stands you on your feet. You slither your limbs back into rain-damp clothes.

You walk the footbridges, two separate beings. Your steps no longer in rhythm. The song fading into the swamp.

Trusting Your Gun

He lies behind a rifle, cradled
by thick brush, the buzz of cicadas
reverberating through the vacant lot.
Flattened ticks crowd the dry
grass around his body, drawn by heat,
by breath. His uniform blocks their way
to the feast. He holds his aim steady
on the front stoop of the house
next door. Inside, perhaps a man sits
crying, the floor littered with bottles.

Perhaps, a woman prays, a pistol
pressed between her shaking hands.
I sit behind a desk. Student essays
arranged in a half circle before me.
I'm working on the C's. Red ink
flows steadily from my pen.
It's smeared along the sides of my ring
and pinkie fingers. Through my earbuds,
M.I.A. chants about bad girls. I slash
an errant comma, circle the wrong "to."

It's an unusual friendship, resting
only on trust. When we walk
into the forest together, I lend him
my body. My faith, like blood,
pulses through his fingers as they grip

my arms, pinning me to an alder tree.
There's a snap when the switch or whip
lands, a yelp. On the drive back, I hear
him talking to his CO. The official story is
I'm not there. In a way, it's true.

Croagh Patrick #8

After he's helped me over a few large rocks, I assure the older man I'll be okay, and he continues on with his group. The climbing is still difficult, but the thing about going down is that, unlike going up, it's not optional. In a way, having no alternative makes things easier. I'm getting comfortable with the idea that I'm just going to have to get through this one way or another. It's a good thing I'm resigned to it, too, because I am anything but graceful as I painstakingly maneuver along the path.

My back is cramping hard because I'm constantly leaning down. Though I know nothing about climbing, my instincts tell me that it won't be as bad to fall if I'm already down low. Sometimes, there are large rocks along one side of the path. They're covered in dirt and greenish stuff that looks like it was once moss, and they're easy to scrape your knuckles on, but they help. I grab onto them whenever I can. When the large rocks aren't there, I sometimes reach down and grab smaller ones, hoping they don't move. Yesterday, I almost fell off a house on Inishmaan. The fear is still fresh. It's not quite the rush I've been looking for, but there's something to be said for getting back on the horse, especially when you understand the risks of waiting.

What I'm doing now is something I couldn't do when I was eleven or even twenty-three: I'm making myself act on the assumption that fortune isn't cumulative. It's random. The fact that I almost fell yesterday doesn't increase the likelihood that I will fall today any more than the fact that a lot of people have hurt me in the past increases the likelihood that the person reaching out their hand to help me over a rock is going to betray me. My crab-like progression down the path is laughably inefficient, but the visitor's center and café at the mountain's base are slowly becoming clearer.

Refuge

Outside the screened porch, yellow flies
swarm. Though the temperature lingers
near 100°, they sense our heat.

I cling to him, my sweat soaking his
already damp shirt. He moves
one hand from my back, strokes my hair.

His other hand holds the leather strap.
Our embrace: so tight I can feel
the strap's shape, a loose coil circling

the small of my back. The wide,
scarlet stripes it left throb. The flies
fling their bodies against the screens,

bouncing off with tiny pops. I press
my face into his chest, feel the slow,
steady thump against my ear.

The Royal Mile

I fly down a narrow, bumpy cobblestone street in the city centre of Edinburgh, Scotland, crying hysterically. I try to remember to keep left but correct to the right to avoid scraping the curb. Cars and people keep appearing out of nowhere, and although I can't see it, I can feel the enormous edifice that is Edinburgh Castle looming above me. I'm driving alone. My sister left this morning, and I have to return the car, but I can't find the Europcar office. I sob harder, becoming increasingly panicked by signs saying I'm about to go onto a major highway. I glance at the tartan coaster on the empty passenger seat, the thin red and white stripes against forest green and navy, recall the old motto, "Fortune Assists the Brave." A few moments later, I find a side street to turn onto and a spot to pull off the road. As I collect myself and consult Google Maps, I look at the coaster again. I wonder if fortune was with me just now, wonder if the courage it takes to drive alone in a strange country cancels out the tears drying on my cheeks.

Croagh Patrick #9

People always tell me I'm brave. They say "You're so strong. Look at everything you've been through." And I think "What's the alternative?" Assuming you want to live, you've got to somehow get through whatever happens to you. Likewise, assuming you want to get off a mountain, you've got to stick it out through the climb down, which is what I've just done. It wasn't a spectacular display of my natural abilities. I scrambled. I crawled. If need be, I sat down and scooted. I even accepted help from time to time. Now, at the end, it seems like that last part mattered most.

I figured out a long time ago that there's no shame in doing whatever's necessary to keep yourself alive. What I've been learning recently is though there's no way to erase the bad experiences that have shaped parts of who I am, those experiences don't determine the future. The past doesn't always or even frequently repeat; I'm just afraid it will. Understanding this doesn't magically make me able to trust fortune or other people again, but it does help, the same way it helps to know I climbed my first mountain and never fell.

III.

Indiana #4

Erin and I have both finished eating. We sip our shakes in silence. She looks up at me, and I decide to resume the conversation.

"It is really fucking weird that you have a gray hair now."

"I know, right? I'm not even that old."

"I mean, Mom's almost sixty and she barely has any gray hair. Neither does Dad."

"Well, Dad doesn't really have that much hair to work with…"

"True. But we're not supposed to go gray. It doesn't run in the family."

"I know. It's really not fair. Why couldn't I have inherited the not-gray-hair gene instead of all this other shit?"

"I don't know, sis."

By "other shit," she means our respective mental illnesses, and the disturbing pattern of binge drinking we've both struggled with. Erin is better at hiding her depression than I've ever been, but I know it's still there. She's also managed to live around the binge drinking in a way I never could, maybe because she's dealt with it off and on since she started college. In any case, we both know we come by these problems honestly. Our list of mentally ill or addicted relatives is almost as long as our list of relatives, and for whatever reason, theirs are the genes that got passed on. Inheritance is, as Erin said, pretty fucking unfair.

Erin's done with her shake, so I give her my part of the check in cash, and she gets up to pay with her card at the register. I stay at the table trying to slurp the last of my shake, but strawberries are getting stuck in the straw. I keep having to pick it up to pull the squashed red pulp out with my teeth. As I fight with my dessert, I stare out the window at the parking lot; the Kroger sign behind it beams like a blue star.

We parked on the other side of the building, where the cars face the highway. I'm sure SUVs and minivans are still roaring by out there, mostly full of people heading home from wherever they spent the holiday. I'm kind of looking forward to the walk back to our car, which doesn't make much sense. It's a warm day for December, but that means it's still fucking cold out, and I don't have my coat. I left it sitting on the back seat of the car. The heat required to keep the windshield from fogging up when we're driving always makes it stiflingly hot. Such is winter travel.

When we were walking up to the restaurant, a sudden gust of wind came up and blasted me, penetrating straight through my jeans and sweater. It sent a shiver through my whole body, and I thought about how much I used to hate weather like this. But I also thought about what caused me to have a change of heart. It happened a few nights after I got out of the psych ward. It was unusually cold for Virginia. I'd spent five straight days indoors at the hospital and was still feeling a bit of cabin fever, so I honestly didn't give a damn about the weather; I just needed to be outside. I walked two blocks down to the river, sat on the concrete steps that led into the water, and lit a cigarette.

The river's surface was speckled with a few lights from houses on the opposite bank. I stared at them and the red glow of my cigarette, turned ghostly by the haze of my breath. I repeated the words "fuck death" in my mind with every drag. I even said it out loud a few times. Though I still felt deeply haunted by the experiences that led me to commit myself, I also felt strangely triumphant, like I'd defeated something. The gusts blowing in off the water made my face and fingers ache, but I didn't care. Maybe that's why as I walked into the icy wind outside a chain restaurant in a nowhere town outside Indianapolis, every step felt holy. Maybe it's why I want to walk out there again.

Meander

I feel myself getting wet
sitting in a cramped seat aboard a puddle-jumper
headed for Texas. I smile, knowing the sleeping
stranger next to me has no idea.
The romance novel I'm reading lacks substance,
but it's amusing to replace the hopelessly dull sex
scenes with my own fantasies. I glance
out the window and am struck blind
by the sun's reflection. Like a jumping flashbulb,
it races from serpentine river, to oxbow
lake, to swimming pool. We're descending,
and every car on the ground is a glittering
disco ball. In the terminal at DFW,
a fit man with grayish-white hair and a stud
in his right ear walks ahead of me.
He cannot keep a steady pace
or a straight course, so I follow
his circuitous path through the crowd.
Outside Gate C12, a group of foreign tourists
is singing "Happy Birthday" in English.
Their voices, though uncertain, resonate.

Thursday Night at the Hipster Gastropub

She's drunk. Showed up that way.
Her hands are in my hair. She pets me
like a cat, and I pretend to be annoyed,
roll my eyes at a friend sitting across
the table. The chills scurrying down
my spine are another matter; private,
like the humming between my legs.
I don't let men do this.

Later, I find her in the smoking room.
Let her hug me way too tight,
feel me up, kiss me on the mouth.
The back of her hand grazes the tip
of my cigarette. We laugh.

Acknowledging a Gift
The London Review Cake Shop, London, 2015

I have four pounds to last the next two days.
Still, I had to buy a cake to say thank you

for the free wooden spoon[1] I received two months ago.
When I saw the jar of spoons, I wasn't thinking

of red velvet, didn't imagine a kitchen filled
with the smell of brownies, didn't taste

the sweet grit of raw cookie dough. Instead,
I saw the cake shop logo embossed on each spoon

and considered physics. Force minus air resistance
equals impact. I've never used the spoon

to bake anything. Still, I had to buy a cake
to say thank you for such an enjoyable gift.

---

[1] At the Association of Writers and Writing Programs Conference in 2015, The London Review promoted their cake shop by giving away free wooden spoons at their booth in the book fair.

Indiana #5

By the time Erin comes back from paying, I've wrestled all the chocolate syrup I'm going to get out of the bottom of my glass. We gather our purses and phones and head for the door. We need to get back on the road so we can be at our aunt and uncle's house in Illinois before it's too dark. As we're leaving—our new charge, the gray hair, still nestled comfortably in my sister's bag—a large family is on their way in. I stop to hold open the door for a woman with a struggling toddler in her arms, and an obligatory Midwestern smile possesses my face.

Leaving With No Regrets

There are plants. Yellow flowers
in hanging pots line the awning
of the screened porch. The wooden bench
we dragged up from the work shed is gone.
Someone's moved in.
He turns the car around.
We go back up the long, dirt driveway.
When we get to the road,
he points out the new black mailbox,
the absent "For Sale" sign.
I try to picture these people, a young couple,
most likely. Sensible people.
They'll replace the torn screens,
set up a plastic table and chairs. I imagine them
sitting on that porch every night.
I wonder if they'd be disturbed
by what he and I did there,
by my struggling, screams, bruises,
shaking limbs, by how he always held me
like a child afterwards. We pull
onto the old, rural highway.
I don't look back.
Instead, I turn to him, ask quietly
So how far is the next place?

Acknowledgements

Thank you to my parents and my sister for their continued support. Thank you to my best friend of sixteen years, Stephanie Medley, for always being there. Thank you, Aaron Lawhon, my friend, former roommate, and survivor of some fucking difficult shit. Thank you, Rachel McKibbens and Jacob Rakovan, for seeing the writer I could be. Thank you to someone I no longer speak to who helped me to trust again. And thank you to my current partner for transparency, communication, and respecting my boundaries.

Much appreciation to the following people and organizations: The Coffeehouse Committee and Ozark Poetry Slam for introducing me to poets and poetry; the members of the Travonna Writing Group for convincing me to write my first poems; the poetry slams and venues of Columbus, Ohio for giving me a place to perform them; the Pink Door Writing Retreat for all my feral friends; The Ohio State University, where I took some of my first workshops; the MFA program at Old Dominion University and my MFA colleagues and friends; my thesis advisor, Luisa Igloria, who encouraged the hybridity of this book; my thesis panel, Michael Pearson and Tim Seibles, for staying on board; the monthly open mic at the Bridge Progressive Arts Initiative, and the Live Poets Society of Charlottesville, Virginia.

And finally, thank you to the following publications and places where some of these pieces have appeared, sometimes in earlier or different forms: *Melancholy Hyperbole, Linden Avenue Literary Journal, /tap/ magazine, Kentucky*

Review, Rogue Agent, Tincture, Barely South Review, Foothill, Adelaide Literary Magazine, Call Me [Brackets], The Academy of American Poets (poets.org).

The following poems appeared in the chapbook, *Requiem for a Doll*, released by ELJ Publications in June 2015: "Upside-down Girl," "4am Aubade," "How to Hide," "Vanishing Below the Waist," "Losing Respect," "Visiting" and "Thursday Night at the Hipster Gastropub."

About the Author

Ellie White has been over-dramatic since 1986. She holds a BA in English from The Ohio State University, and an MFA from Old Dominion University. Ellie writes nonfiction and poetry. She is also the creator of the comic strip "Uterus & Ellie." Her work has been published in *Foundry, Slant,* and *The Columbia Review,* as well as many other journals.

Ellie's first poetry chapbook, *Requiem for a Doll,* won the ELJ Publications Poetry Mini-Collection Contest was released in June 2015. Her second chapbook, *Drift,* is forthcoming from Dancing Girl Press in Fall 2019. Ellie's work has won an Academy of American Poets College Poetry Prize, a Best of the Net nomination, and several Pushcart Prize nominations.

Ellie served as a poetry editor at *Barely South Review* for three years. She also served as a nonfiction and poetry editor for *Four Ties Literary Review* for two years. Ellie is currently a social media editor and reader at *Muzzle Magazine*. She lives in Charlottesville, Virginia and works full-time in the insurance industry.

About the Press

Unsolicited Press is a small press in Portland, Oregon. The progressive publishing house was founded in 2012 by editors who desired a stronger connection with writers. The team publishes award-winning fiction, poetry, and creative nonfiction.

Learn more at www.unsolicitedpress.com.

www.ingramcontent.com/pod-product-compliance
Lightning Source LLC
Chambersburg PA
CBHW020128130526
44591CB00032B/575